Positively
BIRMINGHAM

Jonathan Berg

Birmingham Picture Library 2015

Ring road   Ring road

City centre
Bromsgrove

**Ring road
& other routes**

City centre, Bromsgrove (A 38)

Preface to the fifth edition

There is never a right time to produce a book 'of the city you can see today' as Birmingham is a place of continual change. With the completion of some major projects in 2015 it is appropriate for *Positively Birmingham* to resurface after a break of twelve years, and twenty-one years since first being published.

This is the photographic view of one citizen, who is interested in understanding more about the place in which he came to live. When work began on the first edition in 1990 it was in part the lack of contemporary images of the city that was an impetus. Today it is refreshing to see both a greater interest in photography and often a more liberal attitude to the taking of photographs, partly due to the impact of social media and digital technology. This brings greater responsibility on photographers in ensuring integrity in the images we record and the ways they are used.

This has been an exciting project with many more ideas than available pages. My aim is to provide a means of deepening the understanding of the city for those that live here and the appreciation of Birmingham for everyone.

Jonathan Berg
October 2015

Front cover photo: Skyline from the Staying Cool penthouse at the top of the Rotunda.

Title page photo: The A38(M) connects the M6 to the city centre.

PLEASE DO NOT REMOVE

FROM THE

GARDEN LOUNGE

Foreword

What a great time for this book! Major landmarks are being unveiled, and the excitement surrounding our modern city is tremendous. You can sometimes sense something special is happening, and just maybe 'it is our time'. How appropriate then that the 5th edition of Jonathan Berg's book captures this moment in our city's evolution.

On the surface Birmingham appears to be a place of constant reinvention, but underlying this there are firm foundations. These are both physical and human. The Victorian emphasis on design and the built environment as an expression of self-belief is clearly in rude health. Birmingham is cherishing the old, and blending tradition with new icons. The re-emergence of the Grand Hotel façade is a personal delight, whilst the hopes for the Municipal Bank and Curzon Street Station are sources of optimism. Similarly the 'transformation', an oft used word, but here appropriately deployed, of New Street Station and Grand Central has given us a gateway which would grace any ambitious city.

For me though it's the human story which shines through. This book explores the architecture we know, love and sometimes loathe, but also reminds us that the buildings are merely the platforms on which lives are played out. Birmingham has forever been a place of migration, a place of potential, and above all a place of achievement and reality. Once again that sense of potential is back. The real economic story of our era is the one of individuals having an idea, seeing an opportunity, and making it a reality, whether in a new business, learning a new skill, or just taking a new job doing something a bit different. That's the backstory to this book. With the focus on learning in our universities and colleges, a growing choice of schools, and the arrival of national training bodies such as the BBC academy and HS2 College, we are thriving as a city of learning. That's the best guarantor of future success and the need for a 6th edition.

I grew up around Birmingham, have a home here today and enjoy all aspects of this city – of which I am immensely proud. *Positively Birmingham* created a stir when it was first published in 1994. As you read this new book I hope that you, like I, will learn more about this place, and in your own way help to take it forward.

Andy Street CBE
Chair, Greater Birmingham and Solihull Local Enterprise Partnership
Managing Director, John Lewis

Sunset over Birmingham
From the Spotted Dog pub in Digbeth

Contents

Grand Central

The opening of Grand Central Birmingham sees different city centre areas connecting to form a continuous shopping experience. Named after the original station, Grand Central is a shopping centre integrated into Birmingham New Street Station. It includes a John Lewis store which now gives Birmingham five city centre department stores. The station itself is designed to accommodate the predicted increase in passenger numbers over the next forty years. This major redevelopment saw the station kept open throughout the building work, which included some unexpected engineering challenges with unmapped tunnels and infrastructure adding to the already complex redevelopment.

A Midland Metro tram extension from Snow Hill to New Street, and a fleet of twenty new trams, will link the stations. The tram system will continue up to Broad Street, with preparatory work for this already underway, and the trams will be fitted with battery packs to drive them where overhead cables are not provided.

The opening of the new Bullring shopping centre in 2003 was a significant moment, with innovative and architecturally stimulating designs incorporated into one of the most historically important parts of the city. Birmingham is considered a place that puts emphasis on architectural design, albeit with a predisposition to redevelop on a regular basis. Within the Bull Ring area itself the origins of Birmingham are there to be discovered, with markets recorded around St Martin's Church from as long ago as 1166. There are plans to redevelop here but, for a little while longer, if you are prepared to get up early, you can still see the traditional way that wholesale and retail markets work alongside each other.

∨ **New Street Station**
(Architects: AZPML and Haskoll (atrium); Builders: Mace in conjunction with Network Rail)

The concourse is over 3.5 times the size of the 1967 station it replaced.

∧ New Street's Living Wall

Upon leaving New Street Station towards the Bullring and Moor Street one finds a living wall, with plants chosen for their wildlife and ecological value.

< Grand Central finishing touches

Fitting a mirror panel, September 2015.

New Street Station Opening

^ Project workers prepare for a team photo.

< At 07.30 on 20 September 2015 in a 'business as usual style' the keys to the station were handed from Chris Montgomery of Network Rail to Pat Power, the Station Manager.

< Motionhouse dance group add drama to the proceedings.

> **John Lewis**

Positioned directly above the station concourse with its four retail floors.

Grand Central Opening

< Lisa Williams, Head of Branch, cuts the ribbon.

∧ Comedian 'bellboys' Ben and Ben entertain the crowds.

< Open for business – the first customers ride the escalators.

> **Grand Central**
Reflections on a city.

> **Metro Trams at St Paul's**

New Urbos 3 trams have increased capacity, carrying over 200 passengers each.

> **Selfridges**
(Future Systems, 2003)

The 15,000 spun aluminium discs are mounted on a backdrop of blue-painted concrete.

∨ **The Rotunda**
(James Roberts, 1965)

Originally a twenty-two storey office block built at the same time as the original Bull Ring shopping centre, now given a new lease of life as city centre apartments.

> **St Martin's Church south transept window**
> *(Created 1875 by William Morris to a design by Sir Edward Burne-Jones)*
>
> The stained glass in the church was largely destroyed by a bomb blast in World War II. Luckily, the Bishop of Birmingham had ordered this Burne-Jones window to be removed the day before.

≫ St Martin's has an outreach ministry and a warm welcome to all. Here the craft market sees many people visiting the church.

> **St Martin's gargoyles**
>
> Gargoyles on the exterior add interest if you care to look up.

< **St Martin's and Selfridges**
(Philip Hardwick replaced the tower in 1853, with the rest rebuilt by Julius Alfred Chatwin in 1873)

The current church was built in the high Gothic style on the site of a predecessor dating back to 1263.

< **Bull**
(Laurence Broderick, 2003)

A six tonne bronze of a Herefordshire bull is a much loved piece of public art, a meeting place and an essential family photographic experience. It was recently recognised as one of the world's top public artworks.

∧ Broderick's original clay model for the Bull sculpture can be viewed at the Museum Collection Centre.

∧ Nelson Statue
(Sir Richard Westmacott, 1809)

One of the earliest monuments to Nelson located at one end of the busy St Martin's Walk.

< The Bullring

The floating Skyplane glass roof covers 7,000 square metres.

< Everything happens here and all at once
(Polarbear, aka: Steven Camden, and Simon Turner)

A poem on a granite water wall adds interest on the steps from the Bullring to St Martin's Church.

Hugh Logue Vegetables

The Logue family has run a vegetable business in the Bullring market for around eighty years.

< Buying fresh vegetables in the wholesale market starts at 4 am. Hugh's stall is the closest to St Martin's and is renowned for a colourful display, good prices and cheerful banter.

∨ At 9 o'clock the stall is all set to be worked for the day.

2

2 Municipal Heart

Victoria and Chamberlain Squares are Birmingham's civic focal point. One can start to understand the city's Victorian roots, ideals and future aspirations in this space. The Council House is closely associated with the major changes of the 'municipal radicalism' led by Joseph Chamberlain in the late nineteenth century, with Chamberlain himself laying the foundation stone as Mayor in 1874. The current redevelopment around Chamberlain Square is a great example of how Birmingham is continually reinventing itself.

Victorian architecture, including the Town Hall, Council House and the Old Head Post Office, encloses Victoria Square. In contrast, late twentieth century art installations by Dhruva Mistry are positioned centrally along with Antony Gormley's *Iron Man*. These artworks formed part of a major remodelling, completed in 1993, where Victoria Square became the centre of the pedestrianised 'ribbon' running right through the city centre.

Turning towards Chamberlain Square, the Town Hall offers a connection between these two spaces, reminding us of the successes of Victorian Birmingham. The Town Hall pre-dates the other buildings and has been home to many notable events; from the premieres of Mendelssohn's *Elijah* and Elgar's *The Dream of Gerontius* to important public debates. It was also home to the City of Birmingham Symphony Orchestra until their move to Symphony Hall in 1991.

Chamberlain Square demonstrates the approach to change in Birmingham. The development of 'Paradise Birmingham' sees the 1970s Central Library and associated buildings being levelled to be replaced with brand new buildings. The Museum and Art Gallery and Chamberlain Memorial Fountain offer some historical continuity, as yet again the area around them is redefined. The first components of Paradise Birmingham to be built are One and Two Chamberlain Square, prestigious eight story office blocks which will face onto the Square, and are due for completion in 2018.

∨ **The official opening of Victoria Square**

Overseen by Diana, Princess of Wales on 6 May, 1993.

Victoria Square

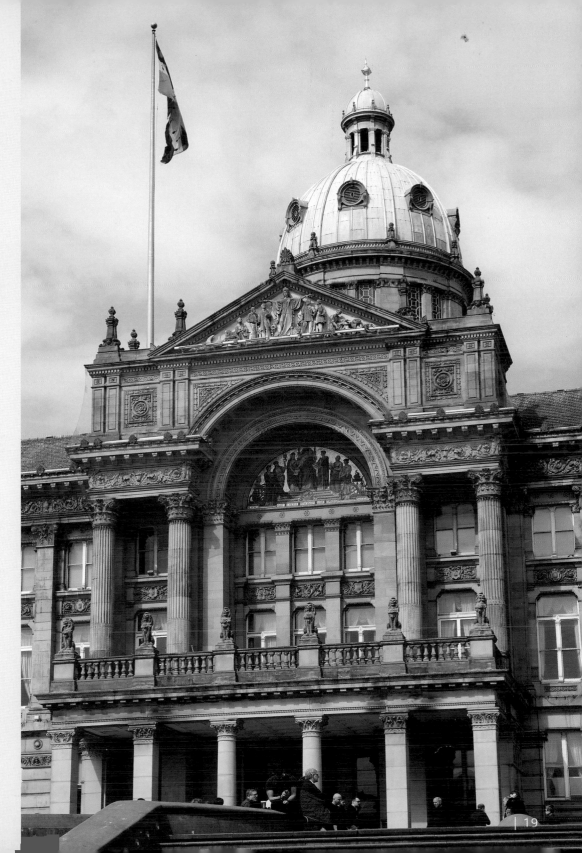

> **Council House**
> *(Yeoville Thomason, 1879)*

The foundation stone was laid by Joseph Chamberlain on 14 June 1874. At the ceremony he emphasised the importance of local democracy saying,

"I have an abiding faith in municipal institutions, an abiding sense of the value and importance of local self-government, and I desire therefore to surround them by everything which can mark their importance, which can show the place they occupy in public estimation and respect and which can point to their great value to the community."

Thomason had previously designed buildings in Colmore Row, but the Council House award was made to him amid controversy and recrimination among Council members. Some suggested the local man had been favoured and requested elements from a runner-up be included in the final design. Architectural critiques suggest this gives a rather conflicting façade with Renaissance features linked to elements of heavier Classical design.

Council House Mosaic
(Antonio Salviati, 1879)

This portrays six figures representing Science, Art, Liberty, Law, Commerce and Industry surrounding the enthroned figure of Municipality. There is a suggestion here that strong local government is central to the success of commerce and industry with Municipality handing out scrolls labelled 'stability' and 'power'.

Britannia Rewarding the Manufacturers of Birmingham
(Lockwood, Boulton and Sons, 1879)

The most significant of five pediments embellished on the Council House façade. The classically dressed Britannia dominates the group, four of whom are workers in aprons and shirtsleeves with their tools and products around them. However, closest to Britannia are two suited factory owners receiving laurel leaves and a hierarchy is clear to see.

∨ The Council Chamber and Annual General Meeting

Since 1879 Council meetings have been held in this semi-circular Council Chamber. The screen is of Riga oak and the panels of Italian walnut with murals depicting 'truth' and 'justice'. The Lord Mayor occupies the central seat on the rostrum. The 120 Councillors are seated along party political lines, with Labour to the Lord Mayor's left, Conservatives to the right and separated by Liberal Democrats and others. The public is welcomed at monthly meetings which are generally held on Tuesdays starting at 2pm.

World War II overflow mortuary

Underneath the Council House is an old World War II overspill mortuary. Victims of the Birmingham blitz were stored here when the hospital mortuary became full.

∨ The circular skylights show the line of the mortuary on the street above

> Frankfurt Christmas Market

The market takes over Victoria Square for six weeks coming up to Christmas, extending right down New Street. Associated craft markets fill Chamberlain Square and run on into Centenary Square. This is Britain's largest Christmas market and a centrepiece for annual Christmas events, attracting huge numbers to Birmingham. Mixing a stroll around the market and chat over a Glühwein, or a large beer, together with a giant German sausage is an annual 'must do'. The Frankfurt Christmas Market is a continuing success now copied around the country.

> **The River**
> *(Dhruva Mistry, 1993)*

The River is a central component in Victoria Square. Mistry described his installations in the Square as follows:

"The central feature is a metaphor for life source. It sits in a sandstone shell upheld by a group of encircling salmon.

White-water springs forth from the hands of The River *and cascades down the weir into the lower pool fountain of the Youth. A boy and girl sit on a cube and cylinder respectively in a mood of quiet reflection.*

< *The Victoria Square Guardians are two large sphinx-like images as composite creatures, carved from Darley Dale sandstone. They overlook the lower pool piazza and protect the peace, pride and dignity of the square."*

< The fountain is not always working; the result of plumbing issues over the years. In summer 2015 the Council Parks Department improvised with floral displays, with tourists seemingly none the wiser!

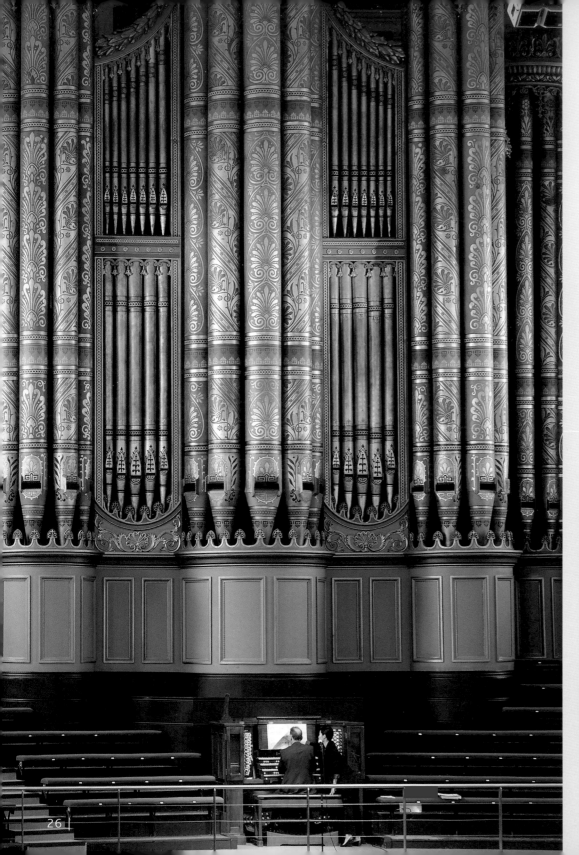

< The Town Hall concert organ

This was the largest in England when installed in the 1830s by William Hill & Sons. It grew over the years under both Hill and others. During the recent refurbishment by Mander Organs of East London the organ was modified in light of the new uses of the building and sensitive to the improved acoustic.

v Thomas Trotter

Thomas Trotter has been Birmingham City Organist since 1983. His regular recitals on the Town Hall organ are built around an international touring and recording career. If you have a spare lunchtime when Thomas is playing he will certainly not disappoint. You can also take some time to contemplate the modern day uses for the building, which, interestingly, are very much in line with the original aims of those Birmingham citizens who subscribed to its construction back in the 1830s.

∧ **Birmingham Town Hall**
(*Joseph Hansom and Edward Welch, 1834*)

Birmingham Town Hall was funded by public subscription to house the popular Birmingham Triennial Music Festival and public meetings. At the forefront of the nineteenth century revival of Roman architecture, it is constructed from local Selly Oak brick and faced with Anglesey marble in a design based on the temple of Castor and Pollux in the Forum in Rome. The Town Hall was closed for a period in the late 1990s and underwent a major renovation, reopening in 2008. It has a capacity of 1,100 and sees a variety of events, ranging from music and comedy through to graduation ceremonies and corporate events.

Old Head Post Office
(Sir Henry Tanner, 1891)

This Renaissance-style building was saved from demolition by a seven year campaign by the Victorian Society. This represented a landmark for Victorian conservation and the frontage adds much to Victoria Square. Now redeveloped for modern office space and with Post Office Counters' main city centre branch located on the ground floor.

v The square is a good place to relax.

> Iron Man
v (Antony Gormley, 1993)

Iron Man is a tribute to the city's heritage. It is formed of ¾" cast iron plates and leans to the side and back. It was commissioned by TSB Bank when they had their headquarters in the Old Head Post Office and certainly creates an impression as one approaches from New Street.

Now world renowned, Gormley himself says he introduced something to the square that was, *"monumental in scale but without the function of underpinning a hierarchical social order by commemorating the great and the good"*.

Gormley says the use of industrial materials and processes in the production of what is based on a mould of his own body, is concerned with the relationship of Birmingham people and their *"place in the world"*.

| 29

Birmingham Pride Carnival, 2015

Each year since 1997 Birmingham's LGBT community surprise us with ever more adventurous parades at the start of the 2-day Spring Bank Holiday Birmingham Pride festival.

∧ The Lord Mayor, for once not the most dressed up participant, starts the proceedings.

∧ Bromsgrove based Someone at the Door Samba Band headed up the 2015 parade.

< Rainbow Voices mark twenty years of meeting together and celebrating diversity through singing.

> Opening in 1969 the Nightingale Club is the largest and most established LGBT venue in Southside, with the city's gay quarter centred around Hurst Street.

Queen Victoria
(Thomas Brock, 1901, recast in bronze by William Bloye, 1951)

The statue was positioned just ten days before Queen Victoria died. Shortly afterwards the originally named Council House Square, was renamed Victoria Square.

Thomas Attwood
(Sioban Coppinger & Fiona Peever, 1993)

This much-loved bronze sculpture commemorates the radical Birmingham banker who set up the Birmingham Political Union in 1830 which asked for direct representation in Parliament. Once secured, Attwood became one of two MPs representing the town.

Chamberlain Square

> **Museum and Art Gallery**
> *(Yeoville Thomason, 1885)*

Built above the offices of the municipal gas department, building costs were covered by gifts from local businessmen and the Council, finding legal loopholes to overcome obstacles from laws trying to limit the use of public funds in such enterprises. Today it is run by Birmingham Museums Trust and contains more than forty galleries, covering fine art, costume and jewellery, social history, archaeology and ethnography.

> **The Chamberlain Memorial Fountain**
> *(John H. Chamberlain, 1880)*

The fountain is central to the square and commemorates Joseph Chamberlain's period as Mayor between 1873 and 1876. The fountain is made of Portland stone in the Neo-Gothic style and includes mosaics by Salviati.

Big Brum Clock and Bells:

∧ The clock tower was added to the museum in 1885.

> **Big Brum**

High up in the clock tower with Big Brum, the hour bell, which weighs-in at some three tons. You get a feel for the Victorian workmanship with iron, wood and brick all playing their part.

< The pendulum clock mechanism, along with the bells, was donated by Abraham Osler who was a local meteorologist and businessman.

∧ A viewing area at the top of the tower was added during World War II and used as a lookout for fires started by enemy bombing.

< Come Forward into the Light
(Edward Burne-Jones, 1885)

A good place to start this short tour of the Museum and Art Gallery.

^ Round Room and Astrid Quartet
> *(Elanor Gunn, Katie Foster, Sarah Leonard and Julia Astrid Wagner)*

This string quartet travelled by train from Glasgow to perform a lunchtime concert in an initiative with Birmingham Conservatoire to bring concerts to the museum Round Room.

The Staffordshire Hoard

These Anglo-Saxon artefacts were discovered by metal detectorist Terry Herbert in a field close to Hammerwich, near Lichfield. This is the largest hoard of Anglo-Saxon gold ever found. The conservation work is based at Birmingham Museum and Art Gallery. Further permanent displays can also be viewed at Potteries Museum and Art Gallery, Stoke-on-Trent, Lichfield Cathedral and Tamworth Castle. Hundreds of artefacts are on display for public view in Birmingham, and the new gallery includes interactive activities for children. There is an emphasis on understanding the conservation techniques and craftsmanship, with bookable tours available to view behind the scenes.

Over the next few years research on the 3,500 artefacts making up the Staffordshire Hoard will offer invaluable insights into the art, wealth, power and politics of Anglo-Saxon times. The hoard mainly comprises fragments of weapons, treasure and armoury dating back to the sixth and seventh centuries. The hoard is revealing much about the transition between Pagan and Christian times. Speaking of the hoard, Pieta Greaves, Conservation Co-ordinator says: *"Through the research we are showing how sophisticated the craftsmen were, this is the best of gold working in all of Europe in the seventh century and will transform how we view the so called Dark Ages in early Anglo-Saxon England"*.

The Staffordshire Hoard has aroused considerable excitement and for Birmingham Museum and Art Gallery provides a fantastic opportunity to renew interest in the other museum collections. The exhibition includes a 'Treasury' which displays some of the more precious and extravagant artefacts.

^ **The Last of England** *(Ford Madox Brown, 1855)*

The largest public Pre-Raphaelite collection in the world resides right here. Many of the works were added when the gallery first opened when local industrialists and politicians were keen to help boost the city's collections with works by living artists. There are over 2,000 works of all descriptions by artists from the 'Pre-Raphaelite Brotherhood'.

This painting is inspired by the large number emigrating to seek their fortunes, with Madox Brown wondering about leaving for India himself. The picture portrays a middle class couple he explains: *"High enough, through education and refinement, to appreciate all they are giving up, and yet depressed enough in means to have to put up with the discomforts and humiliations incident to a vessel"*. Madox Brown used himself and his second wife Emma as models for the picture. The cabbages indicate a long voyage while fellow passengers in the background suggest an interesting time together as the White Cliffs of Dover are left behind.

⌄ The Industrial Gallery

An example of a Victorian iron and glass exhibition room, restored in 1985 to mark the museum's centenary.

> Edwardian Tea Rooms

The museum was opened by the Prince of Wales, later to become Edward VII, in 1885. The tea rooms were refurbished in 2014, and are now branded "ET". Certainly a place of good food and relaxation in the heart of the City and where visitors Raj and Ashok finished their visit to the museum.

∧ Paradise Birmingham

A major rebuilding project by developers Argent on the 1970s library site. Enabling work on Phase I started in January 2015. Prince Charles once said, in a TV documentary, that the 1970s library *"looked more like a place for burning books, than keeping them"*. Not everyone was in agreement and there was a significant campaign to get John Madin's building listed as an example of 1970s brutalist Birmingham architecture. Demolition work commenced in summer 2015.

3

3 Colmore Business Style

The central business area of Birmingham is located along Colmore Row and surrounding streets, traditionally some of the most prestigious commercial addresses in the city. Alongside the significant developments in modern office accommodation there is much to experience, both of Birmingham's Victorian commercial roots and the way the city is supporting the business sector into the future. Professional and business services - such as law, banking, finance and insurance - are increasingly important with regional, and sometimes national, headquarters located in the city. The revitalisation of manufacturing and service industries sees Birmingham growing in stature as a regional centre but with clear aspirations to take on roles rarely seen outside the Capital. Banks in particular are investing significantly in Birmingham and the comparative affordability for both the company and their staff, together with the depth of available skills in the region, is clearly important in the decision to locate in Birmingham.

The Colmore family were of French origin and became wealthy selling cloth. In 1560 William Colmore bought the 'rabbit warren' associated with monastic land between Sandpits and Snow Hill, and had a large Jacobean home built, with Newhall Street originally being a tree-lined boulevard to the house. In time the family sold land for development, with St Philip's Church being an early example. Eventually the family moved south, and from 1746 Ann Colmore sold the estate in lots and the area saw rapid growth. When the leases expired one hundred and twenty years later, the Georgian buildings were demolished and replaced with Victorian buildings, many of which you can see today.

∨ **Colmore Business District**

Colmore Row is the backbone of the city centre business district. This view and the view of St Philip's opposite are taken from the top of 103 Colmore Row.

< **NatWest Tower**
(John Madin, 1975)

103 Colmore Row, the 22-floor NatWest Tower, is being dismantled with a twenty-six floor tower taking its place, along with a roof-top restaurant.

> **St Philip's Cathedral**
(Thomas Archer, 1715)

Birmingham gained city status in 1889 and St Philip's became a cathedral in 1905. The cathedral underwent major restoration in the 1980s and celebrated its 300th anniversary in 2015.

Burne-Jones windows in St Philip's
(Artist: Sir Edward Burne-Jones. Produced: William Morris, 1885-1897)

These renowned examples of nineteenth century Pre-Raphaelite art comprise windows depicting; *The Ascension, The Nativity, The Crucifixion* and *The Last Judgement.*

> *The Ascension* window demonstrates use of simple body forms and strong colours. Christ is in heaven with his followers looking up in prayer.

∨ *The Last Judgement* was the final window to be completed for the west end and is considered among Burne-Jones' finest work. Below the white-robed Christ is Archangel Michael sounding the end of the world with his trumpet.

∧ **St Philip's tower**

St Philip's features fine Roman Baroque detail and a notable concave-sided tower, completed later than the church in 1725.

∧ Eagle Star offices
(W Lethaby and J Ball, 1900)

This is a highly significant building with both traditional arts and crafts and twentieth century architectural elements. The façade features a mathematically precise grid of windows. The building is of post and beam construction leading the way to twentieth century office block design.

> Great Western Arcade
(WH Ward, 1876)

Built to cover the Great Western Railway approach to Snow Hill Station. The Temple Row entrance is the ornate original, while at Colmore Row a new frontage was required due to World War II bombing.

> **Birmingham and Midland Institute**
(*Cossins, Peacock and Bewley, 1889*)

The Institute's aims are the 'diffusion and advancement of science, literature and art amongst all classes of persons resident in Birmingham and the Midland counties'. It moved here in 1965 after its Paradise Street building was demolished.

∨ **Church Street Square and 'Umbra'**

Designed and delivered by Colmore BID, this is a pedestrian-friendly public space.

'Umbra' (*Wolfgand Butress, 2012*) is a hollow sphere with perforations allowing a view into the interior, within which there is a cruciform. Butress says: "*It is an elemental piece forming a link between St Paul's Church and St Philip's Cathedral and which has no back or front, rather welcoming approaches from all directions. A sense of ambiguity is suggested*".

| 49

> **School of Art**
> *(Martin & Chamberlain, 1885)*

Considered JH Chamberlain's finest work and completed by Martin after his partner's untimely death. The School was the leading centre for the Arts & Crafts movement and is part of Birmingham City University Faculty of Arts, Design and Media. Major renovation was undertaken by Associated Architects in the late 1990s.

< The staircase shows elements of Arts and Crafts design.

v **Grand Hotel, Colmore Row**
(Thomson Plevins, 1875)

One of the largest Victorian buildings in the city, currently being renovated by Hortons' Estate with the restored façade unveiled in October 2015.

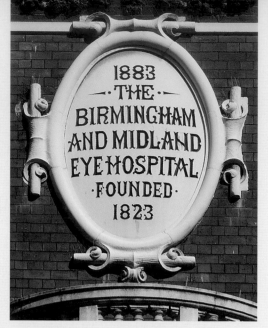

∧ **Birmingham and Midland Eye Hospital, now Hotel du Vin**
(Payne & Talbot, 1883)

< An excellent example of late Victorian architecture. Following the move of the Eye Hospital to City Hospital, the building was renovated, becoming the prestigious Hotel du Vin.

< The airy atrium often sees landmark celebrations. Here friends of Midlands TV sports presenter Gary Newbon celebrate his 70th birthday.

> **Colmore Food Festival**
(Victoria Square)

Each summer the Colmore BID team organise a two-day festival celebrating the many fine restaurants in the city centre.

∧ **Tony Hancock statue**
(Old Square, Bruce Williams, 1996)

Hancock was born in Hall Green and was a pioneering 1960s comedian.

∧ **Bennetts Hill Midland Bank**
(Thomas Rickman, 1830)

The former Midland Bank is now converted into Cosy Club café-bar. Such new uses are seeing a number of historic city centre buildings being protected for the future.

< **One and Two Snowhill**
(Sidell Gibson Architects, 2009 & 2014)

Now home to well-known companies in areas such as law, banking and accountancy.

v Looking down to the atrium of One Snowhill from the eleventh floor offices of KPMG.

∧ **VAX R&D Centre, Colmore Square**

Vax moved their head office from Droitwich Spa to the city centre with the advantage of a ready supply of skilled staff. The 200 employees include 50 R&D staff located at 2 Colmore Square. An interesting variance from their predominantly legal and financial neighbours.

> **The Commuter**
(John McKenna, 1996)

Commissioned by Centro, who include public art in their public transport refurbishment schemes.

Colmore Business Improvement District (BID)

Colmore BID is a private-public partnership, established in 2009, which includes about 500 companies, employing over 35,000 people, who collaborate to improve the working environment and promote the area. The Snow Hill Masterplan, a partnership between the Council and Colmore BID, includes the redevelopment of the Grand Hotel on Colmore Row and several prestigious offices in the Snow Hill area. John Madin's NatWest Tower at 103 Colmore Row is currently being demolished to be replaced with a new building of similar height. Longer term plans include redeveloping the Snow Hill Station locality. At St Mary's Place, around the current Birmingham Children's Hospital, plans include redevelopment of vacated buildings in Corporation Street and Steelhouse Lane.

ᐯ **St Chad's Cathedral and Three Snowhill**

St Chad's was designed by the leading architect of the Gothic revival (Augustus Pugin, 1841). The temporary deer park is to be replaced with Three Snowhill, which will total sixteen floors and be of complimentary design to One and Two upon completion in 2018.

4 Centenary Square and Brindleyplace

Centenary Square was first completed in 1991 with the opening of the International Convention Centre. Now, plans for redevelopment of this 'designer square' are agreed. The most dramatic change in the twenty-first century to date has been the coming of The Library of Birmingham, conceived as 'the people's palace', with both an educational and a community focus. The Library was built on time, to budget and with much architectural acclaim. However, life for the new Library has not always been easy, with budgetary control measures seeing opening hours reduced. This is hard for a building which, as a well-used centre for learning, has found a second life as a major tourist attraction and which continues to have a positive impact on the reputation of the city. The move of the Brasshouse Language Centre to the Library and a partnership with Google will see the building opening 12-hours a day from 2016.

The Birmingham Reperatory Theatre was the inspiration of Barry Jackson, the son of a wealthy grocer's family. Starting in 1907, he oversaw the building of a repertory theatre in Station Street which still exists and is now known as The Old Rep. The company became renowned for innovations - for example, Shakespeare productions in modern dress and world premieres - along with the launch of many acting careers. The move to Broad Street occurred in 1971 with the Birmingham Rep undergoing several upgrades since then.

In 1991 Symphony Hall became the new home for the City of Birmingham Symphony Orchestra and has also attracted the best orchestras in the world to come and play in Birmingham. The acoustics are designed around the classic rectangular 'shoe box' design. Design features include construction using metre thick walls of heavy reinforced concrete, overlaid with dense plaster and stone. Interference from vibrations from the railway tunnel running underneath is overcome by floating the hall on 2,000 rubber shock absorbers.

Centenary Square is to be remodelled in coming years. In 2015 a design competition was held with the shortlisted submissions subject to a public consultation and vote. The winning entry, submitted by Graeme Massie Architects of Edinburgh, was chosen for 'timeless simplicity' and flexibility, allowing the Square to be used for a wide range of public events. As well as adjacency to the Paradise and Arena Central developments, another impetus to

v **Broad Street at night**
A busy place for partygoers.

redevelop Centenary Square is the plan to continue the Midland Metro tram line on from New Street. The extension will head through Victoria Square to Centenary Square and along Broad Street to Five Ways.

Bordering Centenary Square, the Arena Central development includes the site formerly occupied by ATV, later to become Carlton Television before closure. This is a mixed development of offices, city centre living and retail.

∨ **Centenary Square**
Named in 1989 to mark the centenary of Birmingham becoming a city. The Rep, Library and Baskerville House show three phases of development. In January 2017 redevelopment starts, to a Graeme Massie Architects design.

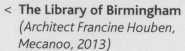

< **The Library of Birmingham**
(Architect Francine Houben, Mecanoo, 2013)

The exterior façade has two layers of metal rings which cast changing shadows onto reading room floors. The asymmetric stacking of different levels includes the opportunity for outdoor public gardens.

> Themed lighting on escalators creates interest as one travels around this ten floor building.

∨ The Secret Garden has great views from the top of the library.

∨ Circular designs extend to the lighting. In 'exam season' seats are at a premium.

> **The Shakespeare Memorial Room**
> (*JH Chamberlain, 1882*)
>
> Originally housed in the 1879 library, it was relocated, after a period of storage, to the School of Music in the 1970s development and is now in the golden oval space on the top floor.

∧ A Real Birmingham Family
(Gillian Wearing, 2014)

Depicts the family grouping of sisters Roma and Emma Jones with their sons Kyan and Shaye. According to the artist the bronze *"celebrates the idea that what constitutes a family should not be fixed"*.

> Boulton, Watt and Murdoch
(William Bloye, 1956)

Birmingham pioneers of the industrial revolution: Boulton, a manufacturing entrepreneur; Watt who invented a much improved steam engine; and engineer and inventor Murdoch. The statue will relocate closer to Symphony Hall when the Square is redeveloped.

> **The Hall of Memory**
> *(SN Cooke and W Norman Twist, 1925)*
> Commemorating Birmingham citizens
> who died or were injured in World War I.

∧ It is built of Portland stone with four
bronze statues which represent the
Army, Navy, Air Force and Women's
Services *(Albert Toft)*.

∨ The stained glass is by R J Stubington.

^ **Birmingham Repertory Theatre**
(Graham Winteringham, 1971)

> Sohan and Aruna (Aashiyana Arts) at the Birmingham Rep annual open day with their Bhangra and Bollywood dance master class.

> Set construction techniques with Laura Davies and Rosheen McNamee along with a 1/25 model of a two-tier set.

∧ The main house sees a large stage and a 'democratic' seating style where everyone shares the same space. Local drama students took to the stage during the open day.

> Mr Toad's costume with Sue Nightingale, Head of Wardrobe, and Kay Wilton from the Costume Department.

< **The International Convention Centre (ICC)**

Opened in 1991 as a major conference and exhibition centre.

∨ **ICC Hall 3**

A versatile area, here seen used for the 2015 General Election count.

∧ **Edward VII**
(Albert Toft, 1913)

Originally positioned in Victoria Square, then for many years hidden away in Highgate Park. Now restored and located outside Baskerville House.

> **Industry and Genius**
(David Patten, 1990)

John Baskerville was a Birmingham entrepreneur whose enterprises included japanning and papier-mâché. His house at Easy Hill was close to this location. He is perhaps best remembered for his work as a printer and type designer. The sculpture represents the 'punches' used to make Baskerville typeface, spelling out Virgil, the first major work Baskerville printed.

JOHN BASKERVILLE
LETTER-FOUNDER

> **The CBSO at Symphony Hall**
> Andris Nelsons' farewell concert with the CBSO who, together with the CBSO Choruses, performed Mahler's Symphony No. 3.

< Andris Nelsons, speaking at his farewell concert, remarked that the CBSO was hugely important for Birmingham's international 'branding'.

v **The Notebenders**
Performing in the Symphony Hall Café Bar on a Saturday lunchtime. The band is supported by the Andy Hamilton Trust, with members from all walks of life in Birmingham and the West Midlands.

Birmingham Municipal Bank
(TC Howitt, 1933)

Originally set up as a savings bank for the people of the city to raise money for World War I, it ceased to be a Council department in 1976 when it became a Trustee Savings Bank.

Saving is the mother of riches!

∧ The banking hall is finished in polished marble with the ornate ceilings offering advice for thrifty savers. Here photographers at an 'InstaMeet' event get a briefing before going out to photograph the city in an initiative by Marketing Birmingham to increase the profile of Birmingham on social media.

< Safe deposit on a grand scale with the basement housing over 10,000 personal boxes. When visiting both you and the bank had a key and 'no questions were asked' about the contents.

> The Ikon Gallery (Oozells Square at Brindleyplace)

Originally built as Oozells Street Board School *(Martin and Chamberlain, 1877)*. The gallery houses contemporary art and has come a long way since its first home in a kiosk in the Bull Ring back in 1964.

v At home with Vanley Burke
(Ikon Gallery , September 2015)

An exhibition telling the story of this significant photographer and archivist of black culture in Britain.

< **Central Square at Brindleyplace**

Five Brindleyplace is the Birmingham headquarters of Deutsche Bank whose presence in Birmingham has grown significantly since 2006.

∨ **Five Brindleyplace atrium**

< The Arc of a Day
(Raqs Media Collective, 2014)

Deutsche Bank has incorporated a number of pieces of modern art in the refurbishment of Five Brindleyplace. This installation in the foyer sees clocks that have words instead of numbers with the day divided up by feelings rather than hours and minutes. Twelve clocks in the arc signify each hour of daylight at equinox and different longitudes. A thirteenth, backwards moving, 'dream clock' marks time in Rummidge, an imaginary city invented by Birmingham-based writer David Lodge. The artwork is visible as you pass the main entrance to the bank.

∨ Deutsche Bank trading floor

The Bank's Birmingham trading floor is most likely the largest of its kind in the UK outside London.

^ **The Future**
(Rob Bowers, 2004)

Celebrating the success of Birmingham's young professionals.

^ **The annual Dragonboat festival**

Brindleyplace company staff teams compete in traditional Chinese longboats with proceeds going to local charities.

∧ **'Farm', Sparkbrook**

Dating from the mid-eighteenth century this was the home of the original Lloyds Bank family.

> **Former Headquarters of the Birmingham and Midland Bank**
(*Edward Holmes, 1869*)

The bank was founded in 1836 in Union Street, with this building becoming the headquarters in 1869. Growing by both acquisitions and branch development, by 1918 it was considered the largest bank in the world.

< **The National Sea Life Centre**
(Sir Norman Foster & Partners, 1996)

Situated opposite the NIA at Old Turn Junction, this attraction celebrates its 20th anniversary in 2016

> The Gentoo penguins always draw a crowd and the 360 degree ocean tunnel is impressive

< Alpha Tower
(George Marsh, 1973)

Originally the headquarters of commercial television company ATV, and appreciated as representing the best of post-war redevelopment in Birmingham.

v Arena Central

Clearing of the ATV built offices and studios in May 2015. Arena Central will see 2.3 million square feet of mixed use development contained on a site proposed to resemble an 'urban meadow'. HSBC are to move their personal banking headquarters from London to Two Arena Central, with 1,000 head office staff relocating to Birmingham.

5

5 Earlier Times

Looking around at today's city we can discern much of how it came to grow into the place we experience today. In Roman times Birmingham was certainly insignificant. Metchley camp, located on the site of University of Birmingham, and the Ryknild Street Roman Road, crossing Sutton Park, are signs of the Roman occupation that we can still see. Even in the Domesday Book (1086) the manor of Birmingham was described as one of the poorest in the area.

Birmingham offered little in the way of natural resources, excepting some energy in the form of water mills on local rivers. However, just to the north was the Black Country which had an abundance of raw materials such as coal and iron ore. Key to Birmingham's success has been ingenuity and entrepreneurial spirit, together with a lack of trade barriers in the form of protectionism from organisations such as Guilds, to take new ideas and working practices forward. Strong leadership at crucial times has also been central to Birmingham's development.

∨ **The Long Gallery, Aston Hall**

The Long Gallery is 136 feet in length and one of the least altered rooms in the house. Originally designed as places to exercise in inclement weather, such rooms entertained important guests with the decor emphasising the owner's wealth and connections.

∨ **Roman Road, Sutton Park**

Part of Ryknild Street (also known as Icknield Street) joining forts at Metchley in Edgbaston with Wall in Staffordshire. One can clearly discern an 8 metre wide raised agger (bank) continuing for one and half miles in the park. Alongside are intermittent laying-out ditches which Roman surveyors used to mark the road out. The road is particularly well preserved as this section became enclosed by a deer park from the twelfth century.

> Metchley Fort

The fort is found at the University of Birmingham between the station and the border with the new University Hospitals Birmingham site. It is the oldest man-made structure in the city. This is the site of a double camp, first constructed around AD46 and defended by a turf and earth bank and with space for half a legion. It is thought to have been abandoned in AD70 and reoccupied sometime later. Evidence suggests uses included a stores depot. Recent excavations have found earthenware from France, timber gateways and a headquarters building.

> Compassion
(Uli Nimptsch, 1963)

Originally sited outside the management offices at Selly Oak Hospital. It is now located within the Metchley Fort site on the pathway between Queen Elizabeth Hospital and the Medical School.

>> The Future
(Richard Thornton, 2013)

Using the double helix structure and in polished stainless steel, the piece celebrates the coming together of previous hospitals onto the new site.

Traveller's tales

During the reign of Henry VIII, the traveller John Leland visited Birmingham and noted that there were half-timbered houses with the parish church of St Martin's at the centre. In 1538 the town was already involved in the metal trades, using iron and steel from the Black Country to produce items such as knives and nails in small forges and workshops.

Buildings in today's city centre that survive from this period are few but include the Old Crown in Digbeth High Street and Stratford House at Camp Hill. The Golden Lion Inn, originally in Deritend, now resides in Cannon Hill Park, though a possible move back to the Digbeth area is being considered.

∨ **Stratford House**

Built in 1601, just before the end of the reign of Elizabeth I, this building has seen many uses, perhaps none more colourful than today, as it is currently kitted out and used as a swingers venue, which when advertising for bar staff suggests you must be of a 'broadminded' disposition!

Ancient parishes

In the thirteenth century there were around fifty hamlets within today's city boundary and the remnants of these are well worth exploring. One can find medieval churches in proximity to ancient inns and half-timbered grammar schools. For example, in Northfield there is a coupling of the ancient Great Stone Inn and a medieval church, while the Yardley village conservation area includes the Old Grammar School and St Edburgha's Church, dating from the thirteenth century. Yardley was originally a farming community and close by one can visit Blakesley Hall, an excellent example of a timber-framed farmhouse depicting several styles of construction.

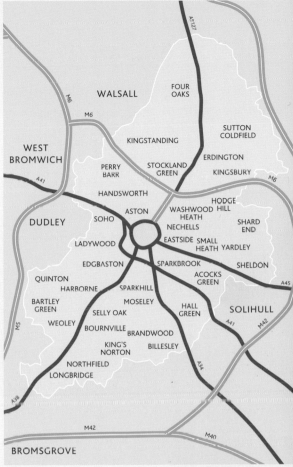

< The Old Crown, Deritend

The only complete medieval building surviving in the centre of Birmingham, the Old Crown is thought to have originally been a guildhall and school, largely originating from the late fifteenth century.

< **St Nicolas' Place, King's Norton.**

Birmingham's largest collection of medieval buildings on The Green has benefited from a £4 million programme of work, aided by winning the BBC's 2004 *Restoration* series.

> **The Old Grammar School**

It is likely that the first floor, with stunning fourteenth century timbers, was added around 1660 to the sixteenth century ground floor to house the extensive library of Thomas Hall, now in the Library of Birmingham. Hall was its most famous schoolmaster (1628-1662), a puritan Protestant, academic and faithful pastor.

< **St Nicolas' Church**

The much-loved and heavily used parish church of Kings Norton is largely thirteenth century with twelfth century chancel windows, fifteenth century tower and spire 60 metres high. It contains sixteenth century tombs and extensive nineteenth century stained glass by Kempe and Hardman.

≪ **The Tudor Merchant's House**

Built in 1492 as a wool factory and residence for wealthy merchant Sir Humphrey Rotsey and still with its original timbers. Part of the building became an inn in the eighteenth century. It was given to the local church by M&B brewery in 1930 for use as a heritage and community centre.

Cannon Hill Park

Cannon Hill was one of several parks donated to the citizens of Birmingham by Miss Louisa Ryland of Edgbaston who hoped that *"The park would prove a source of healthful recreation to the people of Birmingham"*. Opening in 1873, today it comprises 80 acres of formal parkland and 120 acres of conservation and woodland areas.

< **The Golden Lion Inn & parkrun**

Originally in Deritend and dating from around 1520, the Golden Lion was moved to Cannon Hill Park in 1911 by the Birmingham Archaeology Society when in danger of demolition due to road alterations. It is now thought to be holding up the scaffolding that was installed to protect it in 1996! Up to eight hundred runners complete the 5km parkrun course every Saturday morning.

< **The Red Carriage Bridge**

This bridge was added when the lakes were extended along with the carriage ride to the Pershore Road entrance. Ornamental gardens in the park were added with donations of plants and seeds from the Royal Gardens at Kew, as well as Glasgow and Liverpool, to help establish the park's collection.

∧ **Blakesley Hall**

A yeoman's house in Yardley dating from 1590, which is open to the public in the summer and run by Birmingham Museums Trust.

> **Great Stone Inn, Church of St Laurence Northfield and Village Pound**

This is the site of a Saxon settlement. The church dates from Norman times; the pub was originally a medieval 'hall house'; the seventeenth century pound is where stray animals were tethered until owners paid their dues and claimed them back.

∧ Reynolds Technology

This Tyseley company developed a revolutionary variable wall thickness butted tubing which combines strength with lightness. Twenty-seven Tour de France winners have won on bikes with Reynolds tubing. The latest Reynolds '953' maraging stainless steel can produce very high tensile strength with tube walls as thin as 0.3mm.

> Handsworth Old Town Hall

This building in Slack Lane dates from around 1460 and is an excellent example of cruck timber frame construction.

< Hay Hall

A fifteenth century moated house, close to the Warwick Road, is hidden away beside Tyseley Incinerator.

Jacobean delight in Aston

Aston Hall was one of the largest Jacobean country houses in sixteenth century Warwickshire. This was a time when the aristocracy were competitive in the building of grand houses and estates using them as a means of social rivalry. Aston Hall was the family home and estate of the Holte family. Building commenced in 1618 and the house was finally completed in 1635 and remained in the family until its sale in 1817. The house was constructed using good quality building materials; for example, it sits on foundations of iron slag from a local furnace, rather than the more normal rubble. Aston Park is bordered by the Aston Villa football ground on one side and the busy A38(M) on the other. Though many visit on school trips, everyone in Birmingham should take some time out to experience this fine building and gardens.

< Aston Hall
(Thomas Thorpe, 1635)

Aston Hall is considered one of the finest examples of Jacobean architecture in the country. It was commissioned by Sir Thomas Holte who was from a rich landowning family. Sir Thomas had been knighted by King James I in 1603 and purchased the title of Baronet from the King in 1612 when the King was raising funds to quell troubles in Ireland. In 1618 Aston Hall was a suitable project for the Baronet to further emphasise his wealth and status. The hall is open to the public and run by Birmingham Museums Trust.

> The Great Hall

A portrait of Sir Thomas Holte looks down as we enter. As built, this room was not only a grand entrance but also a place for the servants to have meals and for estate business to be conducted. The ceiling is Jacobean with the animal frieze below it added by James Watt Jnr. who made this his home between 1819 and 1848.

> The Orange Chamber

Originally described as 'The Second Best Lodging Chamber'. The dressing room on the left was added by Charles Holte around 1700. King Charles I spent the night of 18 October 1642 at Aston Hall shortly before the battle of Edgehill.

∧ Sarehole Mill

< Before the advent of the steam engine water mills were an important source of power. Originally thought to have been used for milling grain, Matthew Boulton leased the mill for metal working between 1756 and 1761. JRR Tolkien lived close to Sarehole Mill between the ages of four and eight, and it was an inspiration for the Mill at Hobbiton in *Lord of the Rings*. Talking of the then village of Sarehole, Tolkien said:

"It was a kind of lost paradise. There was an old mill that really did grind corn with two millers and a great big pond with swans on it."

Now run by Birmingham Museums Trust, volunteer millers produce over 50kg of flour a week. Sarehole flour can be purchased at the mill shop, with several Birmingham businesses using Sarehole flour to bake with.

> A team of modern day millers keep the wheels turning and offer tasters with products produced from the freshly ground flour.

∧ Moseley Bog and Joy's Wood Nature Reserve

Coldbath Brook runs through the bog and on to feed Sarehole Mill. There is evidence of burnt mounds on the banks of the brook dating from 3,000 years ago. This area was subject to a 'Save our bog' campaign in the 1980s, led by Joy Fifer, when there were proposals to build twenty-two houses on the site. JRR Tolkien played here as a boy and said the area was the inspiration for the Old Forest in Lord of the Rings, and this brings visitors from all over the world to experience it for themselves. The area is now run by The Wildlife Trust for Birmingham and the Black Country.

> **Soho House, Handsworth.**

Matthew Boulton purchased a small Georgian house in 1761 which he extended and redesigned. He installed modern facilities such as central heating, a flush toilet and hot water to the bath, all rather a novelty at the time. He lived here from 1766 until his death in 1809. The house overlooked the Soho Manufactory, just a short distance down the hill and was often a meeting place for the Lunar Society.

< **Lunar Society Room, Soho House**

Includes the original table, used for group meetings, and a number of products of the Soho Manufactory. The Lunar Society was an informal dining group which met monthly for around fifty years from 1765. Soho House was one of several venues and meetings were timed to coincide with a full moon to help with the journey home.

Boulton, Watt & Murdoch

The work of eighteenth century industrial pioneers was hugely influential in establishing Birmingham as a major world manufacturing centre. This dynamic period continued throughout the Victorian era and on into the twentieth century giving a basis to much of today's city infrastructure.

In 1759 Matthew Boulton set about investing in manufacturing processes to produce high quality Birmingham products. He established his manufactory at Handsworth Heath, two miles north of Birmingham. Two water mills, powered by Hockley Brook, were used for metal processing but by 1770 there were 800 workers at Soho, and the enterprise lacked sufficient power.

The answer came in the form of James Watt, a Scottish inventor and engineer, who was making changes to the original steam engine designs to improve their efficiency. Watt came to work in Birmingham in 1774 and, working in partnership with Boulton, over the next twenty-five years they produced most of the world's steam engines – around 500 in all – and played a significant role in Birmingham's industrial development. These two complemented each other,

v **Matthew Boulton's study**

Boulton with his entrepreneurial approach and Watt with a flair for invention, and the effectiveness of this partnership saw many ideas turned into manufactured products.

William Murdoch spent ten years in charge of the Cornish steam-engine installations. When in Birmingham, Murdoch lived in a cottage at the Soho Factory in Smethwick.

> **Smethwick Engine**
(Boulton and Watt, 1778).

Used to pump water back up the locks at Smethwick until 1892. The engine is still in working condition and is now on display at Thinktank Birmingham Science Museum.

< **Wattilisk**
(Vincent Woropay, 1988)

Located outside the Queen Elizabeth II Law Courts, Wattilisk shows five portrait heads of diminishing size, based on the Chantrey bust of Watt found in Handsworth Parish Church. The sculpture alludes to the art carving machine James Watt developed in retirement which could replicate sculptures to different sizes.

∧ Old Mines at Redruth

Where William Murdoch lived when he worked on steam engine installation and maintenance.

> William Murdoch's Cottage

Cottage at the Soho Foundry where Murdoch resided when not in Cornwall.

> Murdoch's miniature steam carriage

This can now be seen in Thinktank at Millennium Point.

6

Victorian Ideals

The boldness of the Victorian era can be experienced through the many buildings that remain. Some retain their original purpose while others have been converted to modern-day use. A number of these face an uncertain future and need help if they are going to survive. During the period of dramatic Victorian growth there were many pressures in coping with Birmingham's rapid expansion. There was a requirement for clean water and adequate sewage, greater emphasis on education and the provision of homes fit to live in. Retail centres were needed to reflect the aspirations and new buying potential of this increasingly successful manufacturing economy. Finally, there was a need for places for the populous to relax, perhaps over a beer or even at a temperance event in the local Methodist Central Hall.

Architecture to express ideals

This industrial town was certainly not the cleanest. Terracotta facings were used extensively for lining both the outside and inside of new buildings. This offered resistance from corrosion from industrial grime and also facilitated intricate designs. The material was produced in Midland towns but much of the most distinctive façades were produced at Ruabon, North Wales where a plentiful supply of clay was a mining by-product. Designers and architects explored detailed Gothic designs which can still be seen today.

v **Spring Hill Library**
(Martin and Chamberlain, 1893)

An example of graceful Gothic design and includes intricate detail. It is now incorporated into a redevelopment with a supermarket.

> Inside Spring Hill Library many original features are retained.

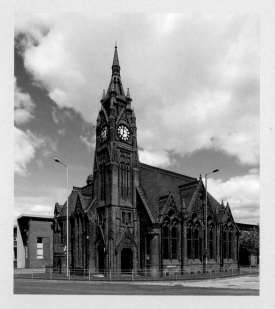

> George Dawson
(Thomas Woolner, 1881)

One of a group of free church radical ministers who preached the Civic Gospel. Dawson, a Londoner, came to Mount Zion Baptist Chapel in 1844. His preaching was too unorthodox for the Baptists and he left a year later, along with most of the congregation, who set up the Church of the Saviour especially for him. At the new church Dawson continued to develop the concept of the Civic Gospel, where he invited his congregation to *"improve conditions in the town and the quality of life enjoyed by its citizens"*. Dawson encouraged Christians, especially those in business, to get involved in politics. Joseph Chamberlain, who was a Sunday school teacher and helped with the church accounts, certainly responded to the call.

This statue was commissioned after Dawson's death, but when originally sited in Chamberlain Square it met with criticism. People felt it was not a good likeness and rather squat and hence it was tucked away in the new Victorian library. It is currently at the Museum Collection Centre with Dawson surrounded by artefacts of the place in which his preaching was so influential.

'Screw King' turns to Civic Gospel

Joseph Chamberlain came to Birmingham at the age of eighteen to work in his uncle's screw-making concern, JS Nettlefold. He helped the company become highly successful, with his role being in marketing and sales. Using new manufacturing processes and modern business techniques, the company came to dominate the world market for wood screws and fasteners.

Chamberlain was increasingly aware that industrialisation was causing major social and environmental pressures. He also heard and appreciated the preaching of the 'Civic Gospel' by non-conformist ministers such as George Dawson. The doctrine assigned significant moral responsibility to the town council and Chamberlain's response was a move into local politics. With his considerable business skills, an understanding of the long term consequences of social issues, and underpinned by the ideals of the Civic Gospel and municipality, Chamberlain and his team set about a major change programme.

Chamberlain became a town councillor in 1869 and, on becoming Mayor in 1873, he laid out plans for radical reform, promising that the town *"shall not, with God's help, know itself"*. He drove forward implementation of the radical policies of the Civic Gospel and this became a model for others to follow. Firstly, he increased the financial resources of the town council by taking the gas companies into municipal ownership. Then attention turned to clean water and sewage systems, and slum clearance. His 'Improvement Scheme' was certainly an example of top-down investment, with the grand Corporation Street and Colmore Row as the key business district. Chamberlain's concern for education is

∧ **Joseph Chamberlain**
This portrait hangs at Highbury.

< **Highbury**
(*John H Chamberlain, 1880*)

The home of Joseph Chamberlain and includes stone, plaster and terracotta in the facades. The architect (no relation of Joseph) was a follower of leading Victorian art critic John Ruskin and used richly decorated designs. The building is now owned by Birmingham City Council and is available for hire for functions including wedding receptions.

seen throughout the city; many schools and libraries built during the later Victorian period are still used today. His campaign to establish the University of Birmingham saw him installed as the first Chancellor, a position he retained until his death in 1914. In all this we can see an emphasis on the quality of the built environment which Birmingham has perhaps more recently rediscovered.

Schools, libraries, hospitals ...

The Education Act of 1870 saw many schools and educational institutions built. The firm of Martin and Chamberlain dominated, being responsible for the design

∨ **Icknield Street School**
(Martin & Chamberlain, 1883)
Located next to the Hockley flyover and an excellent example of the Board School design in a high Gothic style with terracotta features, a ventilation tower and stained glass.

of forty-one board schools. They favoured the Gothic style and used deep red brick and terracotta and included tall towers, and many such schools are still in good condition. Corporation Street is a dramatic architectural expression of the Civic Gospel. At the Aston University end there remains a striking group of terracotta buildings including the Victoria Law Courts, Children's Hospital and the Methodist Central Hall.

... then on to the pub

In the late Victorian era there was a major expansion of public houses in Birmingham. To help impress licensing and building officials, terracotta was used extensively in Birmingham pub design. The company James & Lister Lea, along with Hathern Station Brick and Terracotta Company, included intricate detail on pub façades. Although plenty of these premises survive commercially as licenced premises, a number are now at risk or are being considered for alternative uses.

∨ **Children's Hospital built as the General Hospital**
(William Hensman, 1897)
Plans are now being taken forward to move the Children's Hospital to Edgbaston and for the vacated site to be redeveloped.

∧ **Methodist Central Hall**
(Ewen Harper and J Alfred Harper, 1903)

One of over one hundred built around the country, with the temperance movement offering an alternative to spending the night in the pub. Shops on the ground floor provided income. Services were held on Sundays in the 2,000 capacity hall. On Saturday nights the hall was used for concerts, comedy shows and films with an invitation to sign the pledge as the evening climaxed. More recently the hall has been used as a nightclub and plans are advancing for conversion to city centre living.

< The lamp at the entrance.

< Victoria Law Courts
(Aston Webb and Ingress Bell, 1891)

Located at the end of Corporation Street, this building displays richly decorated terracotta from JC Edwards of Ruabon. Detail is a mix of Classical and Gothic styles with some of the most intricate terracotta mouldings in Birmingham.

> Inside, the Great Hall sees extensive use of contrasting yellow-brown terracotta which came from Gibbs & Canning of Tamworth. The dark, open timber roof is typical of English Gothic architecture.

≪ Birmingham's hidden spaces

This popular initiative to explore the city sees people taking a Saturday morning guided tour of the courts.

< Court No. 5

The criminal court, has an elaborate carved oak canopy. The dock is now enclosed with bullet proof glass.

v Golden Jubilee Memorial stained glass *(designed by HW Lonsdale, produced by Heaton, Butler & Bayne)*

At one end are found Birmingham industrialists and at the other famous Warwickshire people.

Moseley Road Baths and Library
(Library: Cossins and Peacock, 1896 Baths: William Hale, 1907)

v The baths are considered to be at risk and yet are regarded as the finest intact example of a building of this type. The larger Gala pool was closed in 2003 with the smaller pool remaining open at present.

> The Gala Pool, or First Class Baths, contained sixty-three glazed brick changing cubicles around the edge and a three-sided viewing gallery.

v The Second Class Baths originally did not have changing cubicles with bathers changing on benches around the side. Water from the First Class Baths came here next.

⩔ The boiler house was on three levels: boilers and filtration on the ground floor; steam operated laundry room on the first floor; immense cast iron storage tank in the roof filled from a borehole.

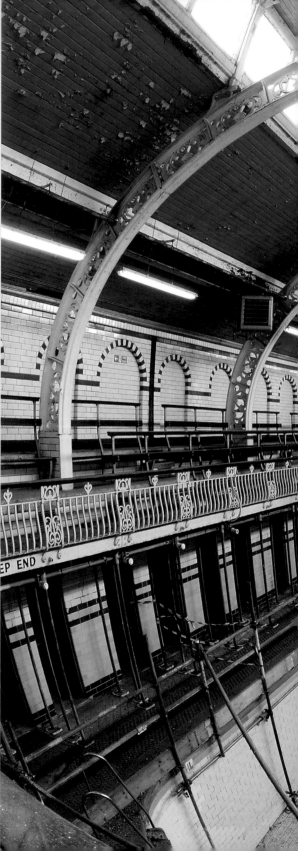

The Bartons Arms
(F Brassington, James & Lister Lea, 1901)

< Built as a flagship premises for Mitchells & Butlers next to the development site for the Aston Hippodrome, which opened a little later in 1908. In a Neo-Jacobean design it is complete with a prominent clock tower but it is the inside which really excites with its original décor and fittings.

> The bar area sees 'snob' screens on the original wooden bar which allowed customers and bar staff to interact without direct eye contact. Laurel and Hardy rested here between their shows at the adjacent Aston Hippodrome.

< The wrought iron staircase is surrounded by mahogany with Minton-Hollins tiles and original painted and stained glass.

<< The main dining room has some fine stained glass where you can enjoy some first class Thai cooking, washed down with an excellent range of real ales.

<< The Bartons Arms cellars used to run the entire length of the building, testament to just how busy this hostelry was in its heyday. Today the cellar still provides the cool damp conditions that help deliver an excellent pint, pulled in the bars above.

< The men's toilet again shows floor to ceiling tiling.

University of Birmingham
(Aston Webb and Ingress Bell, 1909)

< The Chamberlain Tower, also known as 'Old Joe' is a major city landmark. Chamberlain was the first Chancellor from 1900 until his death in 1914.

< **Ancestor I**
(Barbara Hepworth, 1970)
Part of Hepworth's *Family of Man* sculpture group.

∨ Dancers entertain outside the Bramall Music Building.

7

Digbeth, Southside and Eastside

To the south and the east of the city centre are increasingly dynamic areas, which include an emphasis on the arts and creativity, while still retaining traditional industries. Here historic canals, warehousing and industry give considerable redevelopment potential which, if done with sensitivity and architectural flair, can see exciting new uses for some fine industrial buildings.

Development plans for the Eastside area changed radically after plans were announced for the HS2 high speed rail link to terminate here. Trains will arrive, over a viaduct across the Digbeth Branch Canal, at a seven platform station with a glass façade running from Millennium Point to Moor Street Station. Millennium Point itself, which houses the Thinktank Birmingham Science Museum, is now fronted by a city centre park and joined by new buildings which include a major investment by Birmingham City University as they concentrate many faculties in Eastside.

Surrounding the Hippodrome and Arcadian Centre is the Chinese Quarter, known for some fine Chinese restaurants and with a proliferation of café-style eateries catering for an increasing number of Chinese students. Digbeth is a traditional centre for the Irish community and the St Patrick's Day Parade each year sees around 100,000 people joining in the fun along the Stratford Road.

Digbeth and Deritend still have a mix of industrial enterprises, from small metalworking companies right up to major engineering concerns. There is also evidence of previous industries; for example, Bird's Custard and Typhoo Tea left significant buildings to be incorporated into modern day use. The Custard Factory has done much to promote the area as one of creativity. This has been a long term project, starting in the 1990s, and is now a significant centre with a focus on digital and creative enterprise.

Graffiti has also had a dramatic impact on the visual landscape in Digbeth with the 'City of Colours' festival seeing installations added to the street scene each September.

v **Tie**
(Graffitti4Hire, 2012)

On the side of the Zellig, a redevelopment of Devonshire House which provides business space for a wide variety of creative industries.

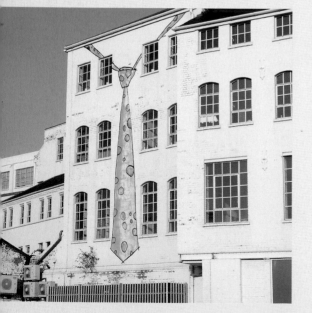

∧ JF Kennedy Mural
(Original Kenneth Budd, 1968; replica 2013 overseen by Oliver Budd)

Originally installed close to St Chad's Roman Catholic Cathedral in 1968 and funded from donations from Birmingham's Irish community. The new mosaic is formed of 250,000 Smalti tiles.

> Birmingham Coach Station
(SBS Architects, 2009)

Refurbished after years of discussion this is also the headquarters of National Express, the largest scheduled coach operator in Europe.

The Birmingham Opera Company
(*Sir Michael Tippett's* The Ice Break, *B12 Warehouse, Digbeth, April 2015*)

Birmingham Opera Company was founded in 1987, and includes hundreds of volunteers from the local community in productions.

The Ice Break included international soloists, the City of Birmingham Symphony Orchestra and a chorus made up of "the people of Birmingham". The highly acclaimed production was directed by Graham Vick and conducted by Andrew Gourlay.

> Lev (Andrew Slater).

>> Problems at check-in.

∧ The crowd drugged out by the psychedelic messenger Astron.

> Olympion (Ta'u Pupu'a).

>> Hannah (Chrystal E. Williams).

< Chorus of the 'People of Birmingham'.

∧ **Millennium Point**
(Nicholas Grimshaw,2001)
Eastside Park
(Patel Taylor and Allain Provost, 2012)

The Millennium Point complex includes the Thinktank Birmingham Science Museum, Birmingham City University Faculty of Technology and the School of Acting.

Eastside Park runs from Park Street Gardens along past Millennium Point and ends at Birmingham City University's Parkside Campus.

> Under the backdrop of the Eastside City Park steel sculpture skateboarders meet, with the water feature adding to the fun.

118

∧ Hebe
(Robert Thomas, 1966)

This Greek goddess, and daughter of Zeus, now lies at the end of Corporation Street, at the gateway to Eastside. She has had an interesting life, having previously been located at Holloway Circus from where she was stolen and later recovered from a Selly Oak garage!

> Birmingham City University

The University is investing substantially in Eastside with the design and media building opened in 2013 and the Curzon site covering the business, law, social sciences and English completed in 2015. The Birmingham Conservatoire's new home is currently being built and opens in 2017.

The Eastside Park canal water feature is in the foreground.

< **Supermarine Mark IX Spitfire**

Spitfires were built in a specially
constructed factory at Castle Bromwich
between 1940 and 1945 and this one
can be seen close up in the Thinktank
Birmingham Science Museum.

∧ The Spitfire exhibition includes
interactive areas.

> **Sentinel**
(*Tim Tolkien, 2000*)

Three half-size aluminium Spitfires
supported by cantilever steel beams
beside the Castle Bromwich factory
where the planes were built.

∨ A spitfire on the runway at
Birmingham Airport.

∧ **The Woodman Pub**
(James & Lister Lea, 1897)

On the edge of Eastside Park is this fine example of a traditional corner pub which now finds itself in a prime location.

< **Chinatown Noodle Bar**

The area around the Hippodrome is known as Chinatown with a growth of authentic cafés that are increasingly popular with the growing number of Chinese students.

∧ Birmingham Hippodrome

Originating from 1903, this is the busiest single theatre in the United Kingdom and sees many touring productions through the year.

Birmingham Royal Ballet

Origins date back to 1931 when Dame Ninette de Valois founded the Company at London's Sadler's Wells theatre.

< *The Nutcracker* is a popular production, often staged coming up to Christmas.

> *Giselle*

v David Bintley has been the artistic director since 1995 and oversees major seasons in the city and an extensive touring programme.

∧ The Devonshire Works and Custard Factory (Gibb Street)

> Alfred Bird senior was a Digbeth chemist who developed a way of making custard without eggs. His son, Sir Alfred Bird, established the Devonshire Works to produce Bird's Custard on a grand scale.

< **Alfie Mo' on the Custard Factory chimney**
(Graffitti4Hire, 2013)

Named after Alfred Bird and celebrating 'Movember'.

^ **The Deluge** *(Toin Adams, 2010)*

Located in Zellig are seven tumbling figures.

∧ Digbeth street art

> Installations from the City of Colours festival intermingle with less official street art.

8

8 Jewellery Quarter

Birmingham's Jewellery Quarter is a vibrant mix of modern day life, 'fine grain' architecture, tourism and city centre living. It all started over two-hundred years ago when the Colmore family, and later Colonel Vyse, sold development land in the eighteenth and nineteenth centuries respectively for residential use. Pressures on industrialisation were great and houses were subsequently converted for industrial use. Multi-occupation of business premises provided an environment that enabled a wide range of trades to work in close proximity; a key facilitator for an industry with many different specialised craftsmen. Extensions into back and side yards and on front elevations provided additional space for workers to rent a bench.

The jewellery industry attracts small business enterprise due to low start-up costs, with a new artisan worker needing just a 'peg' and a few tools of their trade to get established. As trade grew so did infrastructure, with the Assay Office, sources of raw materials and School of Jewellery all still present to support today's industry. Much larger manufacturing enterprises also developed and these included the minting of coins and medals, electroplating and factories that came to dominate the Victorian world's supply of pens.

In the 1870s the idea of putting a pea in a whistle to give an ear piercing noise was liked by football referees who traded their handkerchiefs for Hudson Brothers' Acme whistles. The Jewellery Quarter is still the world's leading producer of whistles using techniques that no one else is able to match.

The thriving School of Jewellery is now part of Birmingham City University with courses popular with international students. As well as the continuation of traditional industries the Quarter also sees architects, graphic designers and media companies benefitting from the creative environment.

For visitors to the Quarter, as well as the retail outlets, there are several tourist destinations that look at the foundation of the trade, with the Museum of the Jewellery Quarter, Newman Brothers at the Coffin Works and the Pen Museum being popular attractions.

∨ **The Jewellery Quarter**

Taken from the top of 103 Colmore Row the sun sets over the Jewellery Quarter.

> **The Chamberlain Clock**

Joseph Chamberlain represented the area as MP and the clock was unveiled by Chamberlain and his wife in 1904. The Rose Villa Tavern is one of a number of traditional pubs in the Quarter. The white building is a 'flatted factory' built in 1971 to house 150 artisans and now known as 'The Big Peg'.

∧ Mary Street 'shopping'

Residential houses with workshops, known as 'shopping', built 1818-1827.

> Golden Square

A new (2015) square between the Rose Villa Tavern and the Big Peg.

∨ Stamps and dies

At the Smith and Pepper works.

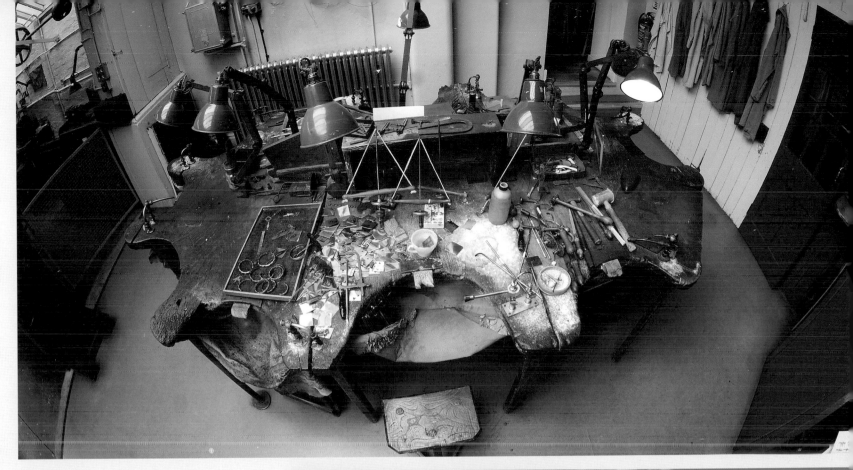

∧ Traditional Jeweller's 'Pegs'

A traditional design still used today with the 'bench skin' helping with recycling of precious-metal waste and recovery of dropped items. 'Pegs' enable eye-level working, with tools and gas torch all to hand.

> Museum of the Jewellery Quarter
75-79 Vyse Street

The Smith and Pepper works is an example of a purpose-built jewellery factory. It offers a fascinating insight into a family business which traded from 1899 to 1981. When the last workers left, the keys were handed over and it is now open for everyone to experience.

^ Turley's Jewellery Repairs

Rob Turley specialises in alterations and
repairs and has worked in the Quarter
since the 1970s.

> **School of Jewellery**
*(Former goldsmiths factory conversion
of JG Bland, 1865, Cossins, Peacock
and Bewlay, 1911 and Associated
Architects, 1993)*

∧ Traditional 'peg' style workbenches are
available to students 12 hours a day
without staff-supervision, clearly
emphasising the ability to work
independently.

< Part of the 2015 Graduate Show in the
oldest part of the building.

Acme Whistles at J Hudson

< The Barr Street premises have been home to Joseph Hudson since 1909.

> Adding the cork pea to the Acme Thunderer 58½.

>> Plating Acme dog whistles. Simon Topman is a world expert on whistles, and now runs the company which produces around 5 million whistles a year.

v The ultrasonic soldering machine where radio waves are used to solder joints.

> Close up of the polishing track for the Acme Thunderer range of whistles.

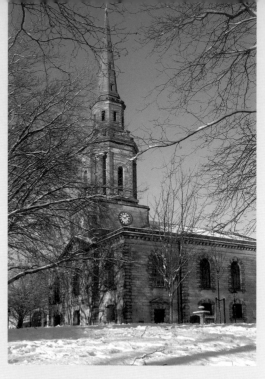

∧ **St Paul's Square**

The only remaining Georgian square in Birmingham.

∧ **St Paul's Church**
(Roger Eykyn, 1779)

Called the 'jewellers church' this was built in the centre of a square of Georgian town houses. From the 1830s these were converted to industrial use, with the well-heeled residents moving out to Edgbaston and Moseley. The church became involved with the much poorer community that came to surround it, offering reading and writing classes for up to 2,000 people a week and opening church schools.

< **The Conversion of St Paul**
(Francis Eginton, 1791)

This fine painted east window adds to the '1240' series of concerts on Saturday lunchtimes with 'Sing! Bentley Heath' providing the entertainment on this occasion.

136 |

< Victoria Works and The Argent Centre

The Victoria Works (right) was built for Joseph Gillott, who used new techniques to produce pen nibs with production at the factory peaking at 120 million nibs a year.

∧ The Argent Centre, built for the firm of WE Wiley, employed 250 people in pen production. Today it provides units for industrial and commercial use and is home to the Pen Museum.

^ **Newman Brothers Coffin Fittings Works**
(Roger Harley, 1894)

Producing coffin fittings in brass and plated metals and later in resins with metallic-look finishes. At its height the business employed up to 100 people. Coffin adornments were supplied for the funerals of Joseph Chamberlain, Winston Churchill, Princess Diana and other members of the Royal Family. The Works closed in 1999 and was sold with its 'time capsule' contents. It is an excellent example of a purpose built metalworking factory now run as a museum by Birmingham Conservation Trust who, along with volunteers, operate tours throughout the year.

> The stamp shop where women generally operated the flypresses.

< Joyce Green (played by volunteer Mary McHenry) worked in the office from 1947 and eventually owned the company. Joyce is remembered as a pioneer for women in business in Birmingham.

∧ Gates to the Jewellery Quarter Business Centre
(Michael Johnson, 1991)

A redevelopment by the Duchy of Cornwall incorporated these gates into a development of serviced offices in a part of the Quarter where the 'fine grain' architecture is clearly seen.

> Frilly Industries

Kirsty and Adrienne are two contemporary designer-makers who use traditional illustration and craft skills, combined with digital laser cutting techniques, to turn original ideas into quirky jewellery and accessories.

v **The Jewellers Arms** *(c1840)*

One of the oldest public houses in the Jewellery Quarter.

9

9 Transport Lines

Improving transport has been integral to the successful development of Birmingham, as demonstrated over the years by the coming of the canals, railways, roads and airport. For the modern city, still very much founded on industry and commerce, efficient transport is as important now as it was for the pioneers of the Industrial Revolution.

Canal revolution

The opening of the canals had considerable impact on eighteenth century Birmingham. The original canal was built to bring coal from the southern part of the Black Country. When the first section opened in November 1769 the price of coal reduced by fifty percent with an unprecedented impact on the town's industrial expansion.

Originally surveyed by James Brindley, the canal was soon overloaded. Brindley's canal was somewhat meandering, perhaps appeasing all those who wanted a 'slice of the action', to the detriment of the system itself. In the 1820s Thomas Telford was asked to take a look at improving things and he described what he found as *"little better than a crooked ditch"*, and set about literally straightening things out. Telford's improvements are well demonstrated in Smethwick, with the deep New Main Line cutting with the old canal and locks above, and with new water feeding in from the nearby Edgbaston Reservoir.

Today Birmingham's canal system comprises over a hundred miles of waterway, important for tourism. The towpaths are increasingly used as walking and cycling routes. Modern canalside developments take every shape and form, with city centre canal frontages including modern buildings mixing with new uses for older premises. However, as soon as one leaves the centre of the city there are many more secret parts of the canal system to be rediscovered.

v Gas Street Basin

The Birmingham Canal Navigations Company canal from Wolverhampton to Birmingham was completed in 1772, and the Worcester and Birmingham canal, opened in 1795. They met at Gas Street Basin but the canals were owned by different companies and separated by a seven-foot-wide 'bar' with movement of goods between canals incurring 'transfer tolls'.

Canalside living

> A number of people live on the canals in Birmingham, with Gas Street Basin itself currently home for around a dozen full-time residents.

∨ Sherborne Wharf is a centre for narrowboat hire, with older canalside buildings now converted to apartments alongside new developments.

^ The Barclaycard Arena from Old Turn Junction

Originally opened as the 'National Indoor Arena' in 1991, this is a major venue for sporting events and concerts as well as conferences and exhibitions.

< The British Small Animal Veterinary Association holds their annual conference and exhibition at the ICC and Barclaycard Arena.

> **Birmingham Main Line**

The entrance to Soho Loop, which goes round the perimeter of City Hospital, with an 1854 roving bridge. Telford's New Main Line took seven miles off the old canal's length leaving 'loops' of the old main line which still exist today.

∨ **President**
(1909)

A steam powered narrow boat built at Fellows, Morton and Clayton's yard in Saltley. Seen here on the Grand Union Canal in Acocks Green along with 'butty boat' Kildare.

< **Guillotine Lock**
(King's Norton)

At the junction of the Stratford Canal and the Worcester and Birmingham Canal, this lock maintained a 6-inch water-level difference between the two canals right up to canal nationalisation in 1948.

> **Smethwick**
(Thomas Telford's new main line)

This deep cutting bypassed the Smethwick summit, which had become a bottleneck and where a Boulton and Watt steam engine was installed to pump water back up the locks.

^ **The Mailbox** *(1970, 2000 and updated: 2015)*

Developed from Royal Mail's former sorting office, which was once Birmingham's largest building. The Mailbox is a mix of luxury shops, offices and apartments together with canalside bars and restaurants.

> **Canalside at the International Convention Centre**

< **The Cube**
Seen from Gas Street Basin

153

^ The Cube *(Ken Shuttleworth, 2010)*
This 25 storey, mixed-use building includes a hotel, roof-top restaurant and apartments. Birmingham born architect Shuttleworth took inspiration from the Jewellery Quarter saying that the gold and bronze geometric shapes make an *"enchanting jewellery box"*.

The Lovely People
(Arron Bird, aka:Temper, 2010)

The Cube includes art installations by the Wolverhampton born street artist depicting real Birmingham people who have inspired others. Temper explains: *"I am measuring people by the size of their hearts...globally people say Brummies are lovely people, so the idea came from that".*

Coming of the car

In the 1890s Fred Lanchester developed the first four-wheeled petrol-driven car, having first tried out his ideas with an engine in a boat, constructed at his house in Olton, and which he tested on the nearby mere. From such beginnings Birmingham's car industry grew, such that by the 1960s the Longbridge car plant was the largest in the world, employing over 250,000 people.

∧ Spaghetti Junction

Originally called Gravelly Hill Intersection, Junction 6 of the M6 was opened in 1972 and over 200,000 motorists use it every day.

^ **Lanchester Car**
(Tim Tolkien, 1995)

Close to the Saltley site of Fred Lanchester's workshop is a portrayal of the 1895 Lanchester 5 hp Stanhope Phaeton, the first four-wheeled petrol-driven car.

> **Olton Mere and Mini 1275 Sprite**
(1799 and 1994)

Olton Mere was constructed as a feeder reservoir for the Grand Union Canal, a purpose it still serves. It was here that Fred Lanchester tested a petrol engine boat as a forerunner to his cars.

This Longbridge-produced Mini 1275 Sprite has been restored by Steve and Tom who, when not sailing, both work for current-day Birmingham based car giant Jaguar Land Rover.

> **Riley Elf**
(Longbridge apprentices, 1961)

The Riley Elf was an upmarket version of the Mini. This cut-away project shows design features and is on display at Thinktank Birmingham Science Museum.

Fast trains approaching Curzon Street

Plans for new fast rail links continue with the development of the HS2 line from London. HS2 is scheduled to open in 2026 and the currently derelict Curzon Street terminus, from the original London to Birmingham railway, is to be incorporated into the new station.

Birmingham Airport is found five miles from the city centre in Elmdon, adjacent to the National Exhibition Centre. The 2014 runway extension now enables the airport to welcome larger long-haul aircraft.

> **Curzon Street railway bridge**
There are plenty of quieter places to explore close to the city centre.

∨ **Curzon Street Station**
(Philip Hardwick, 1838)
Used as a passenger station between 1838 and 1854 and then involved with goods traffic, the terminus for HS2 is proposed for this derelict site.

< **'Take Off' at Birmingham Airport**
(Walenty Pytel, 1985)

Located on the approach to Birmingham Airport the sculpture comprises three egrets in unpolished steel and was commissioned to celebrate forty years of peace in Europe.

∨ **Emirates long haul flights**

These flights are popular, giving easy access to destinations such as the Middle East, Asia and Australasia. The airline commenced a daily flight in 2000 and has responded to the route's success by now operating three flights a day on Boeing 777-300ER planes to their Dubai hub.

10

10 Work-Life Balance

'Brummies' have always known this is a good place to live; now everyone seems to be finding out. There has been a focus in recent years on strategic planning and improving infrastructure. Priority has been given to investment in transport and education with an emphasis on quality in architecture and successful city centre retailing, together with the cultural aspects of city life. Interestingly, and as demonstrated throughout this book, many of these were also prominent at the time of Joseph Chamberlain in the late Victorian period.

Coming to live in Birmingham it is clear that the variety of local communities is considerable. City centre living is well established and expected to increase further, from student accommodation through to penthouse apartments. As one moves out of the central area, the inner-city has distinctive communities. Suburbs and hinterland include everything from the Bohemian appeal of Moseley and suburbs including Edgbaston, the Bournville Estate with George Cadbury's pioneering 'factory in a garden' concept, and places further afield such as Sutton Coldfield.

The continued interest of companies in relocating to and investing in Birmingham is always going to be based on hardnosed commercial decisions. Good infrastructure, ready availability of appropriately skilled staff and the 'bottom line' are of course important. However, it is individuals that judge the quality of city life. Today people speak with enthusiasm about living in Birmingham, with affordability, the excitement of a dynamic city and accessibility all important factors.

The economy and employment in Birmingham is less reliant on traditional engineering than previously. The manufacturing sector has survived difficult times but there are exciting stories in manufacturing and especially automotive components and car assembly. The city's educational institutions are increasingly visible in supporting modern commerce and business and promoting contemporary design and industrial processes which bodes well for the future.

Sport is an important part of leisure time and there is opportunity to participate in a huge number of sports, from the massive Birmingham Great Run each October to other participative sports all over the city. Football in the city sees friendly rivalry between Aston Villa, Birmingham City and West Bromwich Albion and of course Edgbaston is the home of Warwickshire County Cricket Club and the 'Bears'.

v **Inside Tempus Fugit outside Aston University Library**
(Ray Lonsdale, 2004)

Inside the head is a figure of a boy reminding us that *"no man can escape the nine-year-old boy he once was"*. Aston University campus is a five minute walk from the city centre shopping and social scene. The University has around 12,000 students and a clear focus on business and industry related education.

162

The origins of Birmingham's population are as diverse as any British city. Celebrations for the Christian faith are seen alongside major events for other religions such as Diwali, Vaisakhi, Eid and Chinese New Year. The 2011 census saw 46% of Birmingham citizens calling themselves Christian, 22% Muslim and a further 6% Sikh, Hindu or another religion. Multicultural aspects of the city are there to be experienced and Birmingham works hard to ensure an inclusive society, where the potential of individuals can be fully realised. Understanding this, and the positive impact it can have on Birmingham, is key to the future.

∨ **Range Rover Sport**

The latest iteration of the classic design first produced in Solihull in 1970. Still in demand the world over and seen here going off road in Digbeth!

Jaguar Land Rover

The Castle Bromwich factory, originally built to make the Spitfire, finds Jaguar Land Rover a world leader in aluminium car design and production.

> The quality area of the F-Type line includes a 'paint select' tunnel to look for any imperfections that need correcting.

Lander Automotive

Founded by William Lander in 1877 as a wire goods manufacturer. From the 1950s skills of tube bending and welding found applications in the car industry. Today the company invests in the development of people, skills and modern, efficient manufacturing processes.

< Traditional welding of a Land Rover Defender step bracket.

v A clean area for assembly of turbo oil feeds.

v Steel tube is processed into sub-frames for car seats.

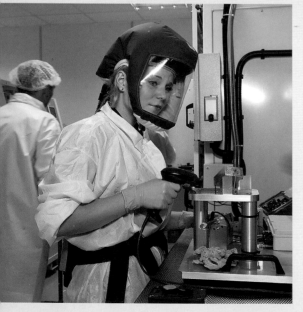

> **Harvey Nichols LED tunnel, The Mailbox**

The Mailbox is a substantial mixed use building including an emphasis on exclusive shopping. At Harvey Nichols department store a continuously changing LED 'immersive tunnel' leads to a till-less store where 'retail therapy' is taken to a whole new level.

NEC and Resorts World

∧ NEC and Resorts World

The NEC opened in 1976 and is a leading exhibition and event venue which includes the Genting Arena for major concerts.

> In 2015 the Resorts World complex opened with its mix of leisure and entertainment activities.

> **Aston Villa and West Bromwich Albion**

A derby match brings an added edge to Premier League football at Villa Park.

v **The Birmingham Great Run**

Around 20,000 people each year take to the streets to complete a half Marathon.

v> **Barclaycard Arena**

The Barclaycard Arena holds large sporting events and major concerts.

Edgbaston Cricket Ground

The home of Warwickshire County Cricket Club which is also used for Test Matches and seen here with the finals of the T20 [Blast] competition.

> **City Centre Living**

Views from city centre apartments get ever more impressive as the cityscape evolves.

Sutton Coldfield

This pleasant district is seven miles north east of the city centre.

^ Bishop Vesey Gardens in the town centre.

< Keeper's Pool was built as a fish pond in the medieval Sutton Park.

> The Big Hoot was a public art initiative which saw a trail of painted owls. 'Spotting and Jotting in Birmingham' by Matt Sewell features birds species found in the city and resided outside Sutton Park Visitor Centre.

∧ Moseley Village

In 2015 Moseley was decreed 'best place in the UK for city living'.

> Birmingham Balti Triangle

∨ Close to Moseley is the traditional home of the Balti curry. Adil's of Stoney Lane was in at the start back in 1977. The recently modernised restaurant serves traditional Balti along with a Table Naan.

< **Birmingham Botanical Gardens**
(*John Claudius Loudon, 1832*)

∧ Still retaining many of the original features of a Victorian public park. Used for meetings and wedding receptions as well as being a good place to relax and enjoy the band.

∨ **Winterbourne House and Garden**
(*JJ Ball, 1903*)

A rare example of an 'arts and crafts' suburban villa, Winterbourne is a fantastic place to visit in Edgbaston.

Bournville Village Estate

^ George Cadbury moved his successful chocolate business to what was then the country in 1879. The 'factory in a garden' concept saw housing designed to be suitable for a mix of people.

< Bournville Village Green demonstrates the concept of providing open space, highly influential in modern town planning.

> Christmas Eve carol service sees thousands of local Christians from all denominations meeting on the Green to celebrate the birth of Jesus.

∨ **Selly Manor**
This fourteenth century cruck-framed house was purchased by George Cadbury and moved to the heart of the developing Bournville Village to act as a museum.

∧ Eid Prayers in Small Heath Park

The park sees some 60,000 Muslims observing the Eid ul-Fitr Prayer which is followed by a day of celebrations organised by Green Lane Masjid.

> The Lord Mayor obliges with a 'selfie' before the prayers begin.

Vaisakhi Procession and Festival

To celebrate Vaisakhi the Sikh Gudwaras organise processions starting from Gurdwaras in Smethwick High Street and the Jewellery Quarter.

^ The Guru Granth Sahib (holy scripture) is placed on a float and is followed by up to 100,000 people processing to Handsworth Park.

< Sewadars clean the road in front of the procession.

> Vaisakhi celebrations in Handsworth Park continue with traditional food on offer.

^ The saffron-robed Panj Pyare (the beloved five of the Guru) lead the procession.

Birmingham International Carnival

Held since 1984, today's carnival procession starts in Soho Road processing to Perry Park where celebrations continue.

Sir Richard and Lady Anne Knowles join the procession in 2001. Sir Richard (1917-2008) wrote the foreword to two editions of *Positively Birmingham*. During his tenure on the Planning Committee and as Council Leader 'Dick' was highly influential in creating an ethos which has lead to the city you can experience today.

Index

Acknowledgments

Thanks to Barbara who has put up with things while home life has been put on hold these last few months. Abi Rogansky at Birmingham Museums Trust and Rebecca Bannister at Marketing Birmingham have both been so positive about this project and have offered practical support throughout. I am grateful to the businesses, organisations and individuals who have allowed me to feature them in the book.

Mike Gibbins was a fantastic critical reader and offered invaluable advice and Raj Garcha and Barbara Berg helped with further proof reading. Jonathan Williams has done a great job on design. Thanks to Samantha Dewey at Jellyfish Solutions and the team at Gutenberg Press for production.

Finally, thanks to all those who buy this book, either for personal use or as a gift to others, as it is only with your support that the project continues.

JDB, October 2015

Jonathan Berg

Photographer & Author

Photo: Andy Street

Jonathan's photographic exploration started in 1990 when he felt there needed to be much greater emphasis on photography of the modern city. Creating images and then following them through the publishing process is something he finds exciting and rewarding.

Coming to live in Birmingham in 1978 to study, Jonathan is currently Pathology Director at Sandwell and West Birmingham Hospitals NHS Trust, and an Honorary Professor in Clinical Biochemistry at the University of Birmingham. His photojournalistic style developed as he edited 'ACB News', a monthly magazine for clinical laboratory scientists that you will not be surprised has an emphasis on photography. For relaxation cycling, skiing, sailing and beekeeping all play their part.

Back cover photos:
New Street Station Concourse with Grand Central above.
Midland Metro trams at St Paul's tram stop.
Bull (Laurence Broderick, 2003).
Aston Villa and West Bromwich Albion playing at Villa Park.
St Philip's Cathedral

www.positivelybirmingham.co.uk

First published in 1994 by
Birmingham Picture Library
14 St Bernard's Road, Olton
Solihull, B92 7BB

Tel: 0121 765 4114

Twitter: @positivelybrum

Facebook: Positively Birmingham

Email: office@bplphoto.co.uk

Second edition   1997
Third edition   1999
Fourth edition   2003
Fifth edition   2015

A CIP catalogue record for this book is available from the British Library.

ISBN 978 0 9523179 8 2

Design by:
Jonathan Williams

Printed by:
Gutenberg Press, Malta